The Cost to Be You in Retirement

The Cost to Be You in Retirement

Revolutionize the Way You Think About Retirement

Douglas W. Fair, J.D., C.R.P.C.

Expert Press

The Cost to Be You in Retirement: Revolutionize the Way You Think About Retirement

© 2020 Douglas W. Fair

ISBN-13: 978-1-946203-68-7

This publication is designed to provide accurate and authoritative information regarding the subject matter contained within. It should be understood that the author and publisher are not engaged in rendering legal, accounting or other financial service through this medium. The author and publisher shall not be liable for your misuse of this material and shall have neither liability nor responsibility to anyone with respect to any loss or damage caused, or alleged to be caused, directly or indirectly by the information contained in this book. The author and/or publisher do not guarantee that anyone following these strategies, suggestions, tips, ideas or techniques will become successful. If legal advice or other expert assistance is required, the services of a competent professional should be sought.

Names and circumstances of the stories described within have been changed to preserve the privacy of those involved.

Expert
Press

www.ExpertPress.net

Dedication

I dedicate this book to my family and clients.

My family has kept me motivated for 30 years. Their love, trust, and feedback have helped me succeed in helping hundreds of people.

I want to thank every one of my clients over the years, who have made my business possible. Their willingness to entrust me with their life savings and their financial future has meant the world to me. Many have become more than clients; they have become wonderful friends and I will always be grateful for those friendships.

Contents

Introduction

Everyone has their own ideas and dreams of what their retirement years might look like, and I'm sure that you do too. Maybe you dream of an opportunity to travel the world. Maybe you dream of spending your days on the beach, or on the golf course, or on the tennis court. Maybe you long for a chance to spend quality time with the grandkids. Maybe you dream of immersing yourself in a hobby, or starting a new business.

If you are beginning to think about retirement—or even if you have already retired—you are undoubtedly wondering how you can make those retirement dreams a reality.

The truth is that each of those retirement dreams has a cost, and that cost is more than financial. Retirement is an enormous life change for anyone, and like all big life changes, it carries with it a mental and emotional cost. What will your days look like, once you're not going to work anymore? Have you thought about what it will cost to be you in retirement?

I have spent my career helping people find a way to realize their retirement dreams, and along the way, have learned how important it is to look at the real cost of retirement. In this book, I want to share some of what I have learned and invite you to consider some important questions as you prepare to retire.

My Journey

When I work with clients, the most important thing for me to do is get to know them. I want to learn their story—who they are, where they're coming from, what matters to them, what their hopes and dreams are. So I guess it's only fair to begin by sharing a bit of my own story.

I was born and raised in Colorado, but after high school I moved to Tennessee to attend Vanderbilt University. I had ambitions of being a professional baseball player, and was able to attend Vanderbilt on a baseball scholarship. After graduation I played some minor league baseball, but was released after a season.

With my dreams of major league glory dashed, I started thinking about another career. I decided to take the Law School Admission Test (LSAT), and eventually got my law degree at California Western Sierra at San Diego.

Once I started working in a law firm, I found that the majority of people who would come into the firm would ask three kinds of questions. They'd ask legal questions about wills and trusts. They'd ask tax questions. But most of all, they would ask questions about their finances. I thought for sure that I was missing the boat because people asked so few legal questions. Of a hundred people who would come to me, maybe four would need a will or trust, but every one of those hundred people needed to understand their finances.

Well, I would rather be able to help a hundred people than just four, so I decided to further my education and become licensed to talk with clients about their financial situation. I attended a tax institute at UCLA and became a chartered retirement planning counselor (CRPC).

I came to realize that I really wanted to focus on working with people approaching retirement, so 27 years ago I moved back to Colorado and started my own firm, Successful Seniors (www.successfulseniorsusa.com).

I no longer work in the legal field, but that experience still helps me give my clients a full comprehensive review of their financial situation. I know how important it is to look at every retirement decision, from Social Security, to income planning, to tax planning, to health insurance and long-term care, to legacy planning. I know how to ask the right questions in each of those areas.

My company is called Successful Seniors because I truly believe that people in retirement should not have the experience of market losses, fees, commissions, or any of the factors that can negatively affect their security in retirement.

For almost 30 years now, I have dedicated my life to helping seniors—those about to retire and those already retired—make the best possible decisions about their retirement. I love what I do and hope to keep doing it for another 30 years.

Throughout the years, I have found that people always have questions, and they often ask the same questions. That's one of the reasons I decided to write this book. These are just a few of the questions I hear most often:

- When can I retire?
- Can I retire without running out of money?
- Can I continue the same standard of living when I retire?
- What do I need to know about taking Social Security? How do my benefits change depending on my age?
- How might my portfolio be affected in challenging economic times?
- How would my family be affected if I were to die prematurely?

- What if I need long-term care?
- What happens if my kids or grandkids need help?
- How can I minimize my tax liabilities?

The answers to all of these questions are part of determining what I call the cost to be you in retirement. In this book, I'm going to touch on all of these questions and more. I will share some real-life retirement stories and invite you to look at your own cost to be you in retirement.

I love meeting people of any age and helping them think through all these important questions. I do that through my seminars, through one-on-one meetings, and now through this book. When I meet a client who's 34 years old and still working, I do everything I can do to help them get on the right track.

But the most gratifying moments for me are those when I can use my experience to help someone who is really struggling for a successful retirement. After almost 30 years, I can often tell them, "Oh, I had a client just three weeks ago, or four months ago, or several years ago, who had a situation just like yours, and here's how we took care of it."

That's how this book came to be. It's more than just what I have learned from my books and training. It comes from years and years of experience, from having thousands of appointments with clients in every imaginable situation.

It all comes down to confidence. When you know exactly what you have—whether it's $4 million or $100,000—and when you know that you are going to make the best decision based upon what you have, you can have confidence and peace of mind about your retirement. That's the confidence I offer to everybody who attends my workshops or meets with me, and hopefully to everyone who eventually reads this book.

So let's take a look at the cost to be you in retirement. My hope is that what you learn will help you to be financially healthier, happier, and more confident in your retirement years.

Retirement is wonderful if you have two things: much to live on and much to live for.

Chapter One

The Cost of Retirement

WHEN I USE THE PHRASE, "the cost to be you in retirement," I sometimes get some strange looks. It's a different way of looking at retirement, so let's talk a little about what it means. The cost to be you includes a lot of things. It's how much money you are going to need to live on when you no longer have a regular paycheck coming in. It's the cost of doing the things that you will want to do. And it's the emotional and mental cost of making this big change in your life.

In my practice, the more people I met with, the more I realized I needed a good, simple way to explain my comprehensive approach to retirement.

One day when I was at the gym—I get some of my best ideas while I'm working out—I started thinking about my own retirement, and found myself asking the question, what does all this cost? I realized my own circumstances were different from a lot of the folks I meet. Because I didn't get married till I was 36, and we had our first baby when I was 38, I had a lot of time as a young man to begin saving before I had all the costs involved with starting a young family.

So I started asking myself the questions my clients ask me. I was thinking, what does this look like for me? What is it going to cost me to retire? I love to take trips just like everybody else, and there are lots of wonderful things that I want to be able to do, like get on an airplane and go visit my daughters at their colleges a couple times a year. What is all that going to cost me when I retire?

Then I started thinking about all the decisions I would need to make with my wife Claudine. She is younger than I am, so all of these decisions will have an impact on her life, especially if she outlives me. I want us to be able to have this same lifestyle that we have now, but how am I going to pull that off? What am I going to have to save now? What am I going to have to earmark for retirement and not touch? What am we going to do about our home? Where are we going to live? What am I going to do about Social Security? It was like peeling an onion, thinking about all of these different decisions, and it all boiled down to this: What is this going to cost?

The cost to be you in retirement is going to be different for everyone. It is wrapped around some major decisions about moving from the <u>accumulation phase</u> of your life—your working years, when you are bringing in a regular income—to what I call the <u>preservation phase</u>.

In the preservation phase, you are going to take all you have accumulated and say, "Okay, I want to make sure that I cannot lose anything going forward." You want everything to continue to grow with no downside. You want to keep up with inflation. You will need to make decisions about when, how, and why to take Social Security, and about when, how, and why to take your pension if you are lucky enough to have one. If you are like most people, instead of a pension you probably have a 401(k). There are important decisions to make about your 401(k) even while you are still working, and more decisions to make about what to do with it after you retire. You might even have an old 401(k) that's still sitting at a previous job. These are all important decisions to make, and they all affect the cost to be you in retirement.

The Three Phases of Retirement

The cost to be you in retirement is an actual number—and we'll talk more about that later—but it's not a constant. It can change. With my clients, I like to joke about the three phases of retirement, but these are real stages.

Phase one is what I call the Go-Go years. These are the first years, as people are adjusting to being retired. They're settling in, they're traveling, they're playing golf, they're playing tennis, and they're taking these impulsive trips when they want to. After all, it's fun to be able to head off to Las Vegas for a weekend, just on a whim. The Go-Go years can be a lot of fun.

But what I have seen with my clients is that the Go-Go years are usually followed by phase two, or what I call the Slow-Go years. People in the Slow-Go years can do everything they want to do, but they just don't want to do as much. They can have a fulfilling life, and continue to enjoy their retirement years, but maybe they slow down a bit. Maybe they become snowbirds or move to a warmer climate.

Phase three is what I call the No-Go years. People never want to talk about that, because No-Go means that you're not leaving the building. Maybe you reach a point where you need some help with your activities of daily living. This can still be a fulfilling time. Even if an illness sets in or something happens and you can't leave the building, you can have some enjoyment in those years. There are a lot of different things you can do.

The key to all of this is planning for each of these three phases, considering not only the financial cost but also the emotional and mental cost. That planning can begin the first day you sit down with me to discuss your retirement.

The first thing I ask of every client is just to tell me their story. Because everybody has a story, and that story has a lot to do with the cost of retirement. I want them to tell me their story—the story about what happened with their parents, their grandparents, their kids. I want to know how things are going with their emergency fund. I want to know if they love their job. I want to know if they see the light at the end of the tunnel in regards to their retirement.

That's when we start to talk about how to accomplish this thing called retirement, and what it's going to cost to do that. Sometimes it involves sacrifice. Sometimes it involves working three more years in a job they don't like.

The biggest thing is to understand is that success in retirement is about income, not assets, and to handle this thing called risk management. Income is very important. People think that they are going to need all kinds of lump sums of money in retirement, but nothing is further from the truth. People in retirement don't utilize huge lump sum assets, and you can't rely on assets because assets can be lost.

Assets can be stolen. They can be lost in a swindle, a lawsuit, or a divorce. They can be disseminated in an accident. What people really need to understand is their income. This cost to be you in retirement boils down into what you can do now to afford this thing called retirement by utilizing income.

Among the thousands of clients that I've dealt with over the years, very few people have ever come to me and said, "Hey, you know what? I need a lump sum of money." People come to me and they say, "Hey, is there any way that we can get a little bit more income? We've done great over the last five years of retirement, but we can use a little bit more income."

Another important piece of the cost to be you in retirement, and one that is often overlooked, is longevity. People are living longer, and thanks to ongoing medical advancements, your lifespan may be significantly longer than you expect. You must have a plan for that.

Life expectancies vary among spouses and genders, and it's beneficial to plan for the longer of your two life expectancies between you and your spouse or partner. Research says that on average, women live five years longer than men, and about 85 percent of the time, men die before women. So it's important to understand that the cost to be you in retirement is the cost for both you and your partner. No one wants to be impoverished later in life because they lived longer than they expected. If you have a spouse or partner, you should both prepare to live a long time, and make sure you have enough money to maintain your lifestyle. What is the cost to be both of you in retirement?

Cost is More Than Money

Working with hundreds and hundreds of retirees over the years has shown me how important it is to understand that the cost to be you in retirement is not just financial.

You probably have some idea of what your retirement will look like or what you're going to do once you retire. It may be as simple as thinking, "Oh, it's going to be so great not to have to go to work anymore." Then the day actually arrives, and you find out that retirement is not necessarily what you thought it was going to be.

When you're working, that's taking probably 10 hours of your day, every day. Think about it: say an hour to get ready and get to work, eight hours on the job, and then another hour to get home. So you retire and you start out having a lot more free time, and then after a few weeks you discover that you're really bored. Maybe you start to think, "Now I want to go do something else." That can change the cost to be you in retirement.

One of my best examples of this was my own dad. My dad and I played 20 years of golf league together, every Thursday night for a good part of the year. When he retired I worried that he would get bored. I thought he would probably want to play golf a lot more than once a week. The funny thing was that my dad kept so busy in retirement there were times when I didn't think he would even have time to play in golf league anymore.

There are so many things you can do in retirement that you may never have imagined. I always tell my clients that they have a safety net to guard against getting bored in retirement. You can find some kind of fun job, something completely different from the daily grind.

For instance, I still love to watch baseball. There's a minor league team here where I live, and when I go to these games, I see lots of seniors working at the ballpark. They may be ushering or working at concessions, but they're out working two or three times a week for a few hours. When I see them at the ballpark, they're smiling, they're having fun, and they get a little bit of spending money.

Here's another example. How often do you go to Sam's or Costco and see people doing recipe demonstrations or offering food samples? These folks are often retirees who have the opportunity to get out of the house, have some fun, and make a little bit of spending money.

People have so many different options. Maybe they didn't get to enjoy that gym membership while they were working. When I go to the gym these days, I would guess that 70 percent or more of the people I see there are 60 and older. It's not a gym full of 24-year-olds. It's a gym full of people who are doing and enjoying the exercise that they didn't get to do during their working years. Boredom in retirement is a real thing and it's an emotional thing. It can be horrible. Letting go of a familiar daily routine can be difficult and emotional. One of the best ways to deal with the emotional cost of retirement is anticipation and proper planning. One of the things I offer my clients is my experience from walking hundreds of clients through not just the financial side of retirement but also the mental and emotional challenges.

I ask them to start envisioning what it's going to be like every morning. Do they realize they're going to have an additional hour to read the paper, an additional half hour to drink a little bit more coffee, to get their day jump-started and decide what they're going to do? It helps in making that mental adjustment.

For instance, people will tell me that they want to do some volunteer work when they retire, or they want to get involved in one thing or another. They ask me for recommendations, and I can tell them about four people who are volunteering down at the hospital, or six people doing other charitable things in the community. I have clients who are involved in various car clubs and I can't believe how busy they stay with those. I have several clients who are Shriners, which is a wonderful organization that does so much good. I love seeing clients able to enjoy their retirement spending hours doing all of these wonderful things that they didn't have time to do while they were working.

I tell my clients—and I truly believe this—that it's going to be a wonderful time in their life.

Now there is another mental piece about retirement, and that is the reality of aging. No one is immune to that. I think it hits everyone at some point. For some, it's at 50 or 60; for others it doesn't hit until they actually retire. For me, the reality of aging never hit until the day I turned 50. I didn't handle it well; I found I had to take my own advice about looking at the prospect of retirement. It was a bit of a mental adjustment to realize I had to start figuring out what it would cost me to be myself in my own retirement.

One of the things that helped me was this quote: "Aging is a privilege that is not enjoyed by everyone." It's true. Not everyone gets to enjoy their old age.

My dad, for example, worked 40 years in a steel mill. My mom worked those 40 years alongside him. But my dad didn't get to enjoy his retirement for long; he passed away when he was just over 70. He was a great role model, though. In his few short years of retirement, he filled up every single day.

Think about your typical day. On an average day, it seems to me, I get up and get a few things done, then I work and all of a sudden I look at the clock and it's three, then I look again and all of a sudden it's six thirty. I go home, have dinner, and spend a little time with my family. Before I know it the day is over and I'm wondering where it went. Does that sound familiar? Now think about what that day will look like once you retire.

It's one thing to envision that typical day in retirement, but it's another to make it a reality. To do that, you need to start thinking about why, when, and how to retire. The truth is that most people procrastinate about planning for their retirement. They have all kinds of reasons for putting it off. Maybe the prospect is too overwhelming. Maybe there are too many decisions to make. Maybe they're afraid they will run out of money. They get frustrated because they have all these goals but they can't pull them all together.

That's where I come in. My goal is to help them—and help you—by simplifying this frustrating process. If I can help them look realistically at the cost of retirement, they can get to a transition point where they can make those decisions about why, when, and how to retire.

It happens over and over again. I'll tell someone, "Hey, you've paid your dues with the decisions that you need to make with Social Security, your pension and your savings. Now look at what you can make in retirement." I show them the result on my financial calculator, and they say, "Well, why would I not retire?"

It's all about planning. Just a couple of weeks ago I was having pizza with my clients Bob and Ellen. I explained a little bit about what they could potentially have for income in their retirement, then I turned my financial calculator to show them the figures. It was amazing. Ellen looked at me and said, "Well, why wouldn't we do that in five years?" And I said, "Why wouldn't you?"

One more thing is that you don't need to quit your job. Ellen does some part-time delivery work that she really loves. She told me a story about a horse that she gets to drive by every day that loves peppermint candy. When the weather's nice, and she drives around this one corner, the horse sees her truck and comes to the gate. Ellen gets out of her truck and gives the horse a piece of peppermint candy. It's a highlight of her day. I thought it was one of the coolest things I'd ever heard in my life. Why would she ever want to stop doing that if she enjoys it so much?

Retiring doesn't mean that you are going to run across a finish line, fall on your knees in exhaustion, and then you're done. What really happens when you retire and you cross that finish line is that you face a whole new challenge. But with planning you're going to be able to face that challenge by building upon everything that you have already done. When you know the cost to be you in retirement, you can move forward without the financial pressure and without the regret that can age you faster than anything else. And you're going to be able to check off some of those items on your bucket list.

It is not true that people stop pursuing dreams because they grow old—they grow old because they stop pursuing dreams.

Chapter Two

Why Retire?

YOU MIGHT BE SURPRISED to see the title of this chapter, but I believe the "why" part of retiring is very important. Of course, the "when" and the "how" are critical, and practical, and we're going to dive deeper into those in the following chapters. But the nuts and bolts of how and when only make sense when you know exactly why you want to retire.

So, have you really thought about <u>why</u> you want to retire? Or even <u>if</u> you want to retire?

The word retirement means different things to different people. Some people just want to stop working completely. Some want to continue working part time, or maybe try something new. Some people want to play more golf; some people want to play more tennis; some people want to travel more.

So that's the key question you need to ask yourself here. What does retirement mean to you?

The Perils of Procrastination

Whatever your idea of retirement, there's no denying that it means a big change in your life. And unfortunately, what most people do with the prospect of such a major life change is procrastinate. But the longer you procrastinate, the more you risk finding yourself with your back against the wall, forced to make decisions for which you are unprepared.

Some of my toughest appointments are those when I have to explain to people that by having procrastinated for years, it may take a little bit longer to be able to buy that boat, or take that cruise, or do all the things they want to do with their grandkids.

I understand that change is difficult. I understand how tempting it can be to procrastinate. One of the things I bring to my clients is a willingness to call them out a bit when I sense that they're procrastinating. I can be pretty adamant about telling them, "You know, these are things that we need to do today." It may be uncomfortable, but I believe it's one of the most important ways that I serve my clients, by helping them get past that hurdle of procrastination so that they can have an actual plan.

I find that for the most part, people really just want to be able to catch their breath and settle into a safe and secure retirement. They don't want to be fretting about the stock market, or worrying about paying fees and commissions. They basically just want to be able to put things on cruise control.

That's where I come in. Through my experience, I show my clients that if they put things in place three to four years before they retire, they can have the security they want. But if they don't—if they keep procrastinating—then we can find ourselves having to put out a succession of fires and hoping that things can still fall in place. It's the critical difference between planning proactively and responding reactively.

The Bucket List

This is what I tell people at the beginning of all my workshops: I believe there are only two things that age people—regret and financial pressure. With proper planning for your retirement, you can avoid both of those things.

In my experience, I often find that people want to retire because they feel they've paid their dues.

They usually have a bucket list of things that they want to do or accomplish, but most of them have not thought about how to make that list a reality.

Because I think it's so important to think through these questions, I actually give my clients a little notebook that says "Bucket List" on top. I ask them to write down the things that they want to do in their retirement, and then to prioritize the things on that list.

Maybe the number one item on their bucket list is a cruise around the world. That's great, and I will take that into account as I help them examine their priorities and their resources. When people actually look at their bucket list on paper, they often find their priorities shift.

When I begin working with a client, I want to get know them. I invite them to visualize what their typical day in retirement might be and to do that I need to know what motivates them.

Let me use my own life as an example. I'm many years from retirement, but I have to constantly ask myself what will motivate me this week or this month to do the things I need to do in order to reach my goals and get closer to retirement. I am always motivated by the fact that every day I get to help people and see them smile. And in my personal life, what motivates me is the next trip to see my girls in college, and the smile on my wife's face when we get to go experience something that we've never done before. We love to do new things. And believe it or not, I also get motivated by yard work. I love yard work. I look forward every year to doing a few different things in my yard that I didn't do the year before.

So maybe a retiree has always wanted time to plant that garden, something that would let them grow their own herbs, lettuce, and carrots. Or maybe they just want to be able to jump on a plane once a month and travel somewhere. Those goals and motivations will be different for everyone.

That's why I want to really understand my clients' goals and priorities so that I can help them create a road map that will get them to those goals.

I want to be clear that the goals are not mine; they are always the client's goals, but it's important for me to understand them. Sometimes I think I've heard almost every goal imaginable. I've had people decide that they want to start raising dogs. I've had people decide that they're going to move to another country. But with the proper planning, I've been able to help them reach all those goals.

For example, let me tell you about Mike. He used to go to the beach all the time, where he would sit on the shore and stare at the boats. He always wanted to be able to go ocean fishing. Well, how was he going to do that? He certainly didn't want to rent a boat every time he went out, but he wanted to be able to spend months at a time in other places. With planning and with the amount of money that he had in his various accounts, we were able to make a plan for Mike to reach his goal. Now he has his own boat, based in Mexico—in Cabo—which makes it really affordable. He's able to maintain the boat and spend a lot of time down there. And he's not just sitting on the shore anymore.

Mike's story is a good example because it shows that your goals may be more affordable and attainable than you think they are. It sounds unbelievable, but people often overestimate the cost and underestimate their ability to do what they want to do in retirement. Sometimes being frugal in one area opens up possibilities in another. Don't be afraid to dream about what you want to do, and don't wait too long.

As I said before, regret ages people. Let's find a way for you to do the things you want to do in your retirement before it's too late and you're no longer physically able to do them. Because when you get to the No-Go phase, you're not leaving the building. You don't want wait too long and then look back in regret, saying, "We had all those years while we were able to walk, move, maneuver the boat and do all those things, but we can't do those things now."

So think about it. What are your goals? Why do you want to retire?

Age is an issue of mind over matter.
If you don't mind, it doesn't matter.

Chapter Three

When to Retire?

Now that you've thought about why you want to retire, and what you want your retirement to look like, it's time to think about when to retire.

The timing of your retirement is another big decision, and there are a number of factors to consider. Look at it this way: Retirement is the longest period of unemployment in your entire lifetime. You are no longer in the accumulation phase of your financial life; you are in the preservation phase.

Yes, you still need to make money on your money, but your focus needs to be preserving what you have. That being said, there are four things you cannot afford in retirement:

- You can't afford market losses.

- You can't afford paying someone a fee to help you.

- You can't afford paying a commission to somebody to help you.

- You can't be in the wrong income plan.

Your income plan is the biggest thing. Once you retire, you need regular income to take the place of your weekly or monthly paycheck. It's a very common misunderstanding, but people in retirement don't need lump sums; they need income, and a plan to maintain that income.

How Long Does Your Money Need to Last?

The number one fear among people approaching retirement is the fear of outliving their money, and not having a plan increases the risk of doing just that.

When I talk about outliving your money, I'm not talking about becoming homeless. What I am talking about is not being able to do the things you want to do or live the way you want in your retirement years. By figuring out the cost to be you in your retirement, we can make a plan so that you can let go of that fear.

Statistics show that people are living longer now than ever before, but in my experience, most people underestimate their longevity. I hear it all the time: "Oh, with my family history I'll be lucky to make it to 70." But we all know people in their 80s and even 90s who are living full, active lives.

Heredity is only one aspect of longevity. What's going to happen is going to happen, but taking care of yourself physically and maintaining a healthy lifestyle make a difference, along with the many advances in medicine that have happened since our parents' time.

Speaking of medicine, right behind the fear of outliving one's money comes the fear of having to go into a nursing home or assisted living. Proper planning can help you be prepared if that day comes.

It Takes Two

If you have a spouse or partner, your retirement isn't just about you. These are decisions that you need to discuss and make together, because the results will affect both of you.

I'm always amazed by how many spouses tell me, "Oh, we've never really talked about that." The two of you need to get on the same page as you approach retirement. I've seen it in my own life; I realized that my wife's concerns about retirement are very different from mine and we have to keep talking about those things.

How Do You Decide When to Retire?

There are several key factors that can influence the timing of your retirement, such as your pension, your Social Security, your savings, and long-term care needs. Let's look at each of these a little more closely.

Pensions

When my grandpa Hank retired after 40 years as an engineer, the company gave him three things: a party, a gold watch, and a pension. He was lucky; his pension extended for his lifetime and also for my grandma's life after he passed. Most workers today are not as fortunate, and whether or not you have a pension can have a big effect on when you might choose to retire.

If you are lucky enough to have a pension—most Americans don't—then you have important decisions to make about how you take that pension. It doesn't just happen automatically.

When you receive a pension, you generally have to choose among three options. The first thing they ask is if you want to keep 100 percent of your pension. Well, who would say no to that? Of course you want to keep all of your pension. But the next question is about whether you want to take a spousal benefit. The options for spousal benefits can vary, but here's a typical example: You defer 25 percent of your pension amount so that your spouse will continue to receive your pension if you pass away first. And of course you want to provide for your spouse. But what if your spouse passes away first? Who keeps the 25 percent that you deferred? You guessed it—the company keeps it. You certainly don't get it back. Do the math—how does 25 percent of your pension add up over time?

When I work with clients who have a pension, I show them that we can make other plans that will provide for their spouse and still allow them to keep 100 percent of their pension. I had this very conversation with my own dad. When I asked him how much time he had spent working, he said, "41 years, three weeks, two days, and six hours." He had it down to the very day. So I said, "Dad, you are so organized with all this. Why would you make a decision that allows that company to keep the money?"

Social Security

For many retirees, especially those without pensions, Social Security is a big piece of their retirement income. Given that it provides a lifetime monthly check, it may be the closest thing these people have to a pension. And just as with a pension, it doesn't start automatically. There are many decisions to make about your Social Security.

I have taught Social Security classes for years, and one of the things I've found is that while most people think they understand Social Security, they are usually mistaken. There are many options to consider. For example:

- When should you start taking Social Security?
- What are the catches you need to understand about Social Security?
- Can you take Social Security and still continue to work?
- How do your Social Security decisions affect your spouse?
- What are the tax implications?

When should you start taking Social Security? Ideally, everyone should wait at least until their full retirement age, which is now 67 for people born in 1960 or later. Yes, you can start taking Social Security at age 62, but your benefit will be lower and you will be limited in what you can make if you continue working.

In counseling people, I explain to them that they can start taking Social Security at age 62 or defer it all the way up to age 70, and I show them what will happen with their Social Security each year. If you defer your Social Security past your full retirement age, your benefit will increase by eight percent a year until you reach age 70, when you have to take it.

As with a pension, the decisions you make about your Social Security also affect your spouse. Suppose a husband and wife are both retired and collecting Social Security. When one spouse passes away, the surviving spouse gets only the larger of the two monthly checks, not both. That can mean a huge drop in household income for the survivor. That's something to keep in mind as you both decide when to start taking Social Security. If you take it before your full retirement age, you lock in that reduced benefit amount, so you need to consider what kind of a benefit you would be leaving for your spouse.

It's also important to note that your Social Security benefit is now taxable up to 85 percent, but as we put together your retirement plan we can work to avoid that tax.

Savings

As you consider when to retire, you also have to look at your savings. The average bank account today only pays about 0.13 percent. People who are retired today have retired at some of the lowest interest rates in our country's history. How are you going to keep pace with inflation when your money is only returning 0.13 percent?

I find that baby boomers tend to keep a pretty large emergency fund, most likely because they have experienced times when they didn't have a lot of money in the bank and they feel that insecurity again. And of course I always advise keeping an emergency fund in the bank; it's a liquid asset that you can access immediately in an emergency. The recommended amount for your emergency fund will depend on your own circumstances and it will be different for everyone.

But apart from that, there are options that can put some of your money to work for you—without downside risk—and still maintain tremendous liquidity. I help my clients to understand what the money in the bank is doing and how it fits into the jigsaw puzzle of their retirement plan, which includes all of the pieces we've talked about here.

A lot of my clients are using their savings to deal with the issue of long-term care, which is another challenge in itself.

Long-Term Care: What You Need to Know

Chances are you, your spouse, or someone in your family will eventually need long-term care.

What you may not realize is that long-term care is not covered by Medicare or by your health insurance. That means you need a plan.

When I mention long-term care, most people think first about traditional long-term care insurance. But because people are living so much longer, long-term care insurance is very expensive and is becoming harder and harder to get. Four of the largest insurance companies have recently stopped selling long-term care insurance altogether, and one of the biggest current sellers of long-term care insurance has been raising its premiums 28 percent a year. Along with all that, making a claim on a long-term care policy can be a miserable business. It's like trying to prove that you are permanently disabled. I know this well, because some of my biggest frustrations have come when I have tried to help clients make those claims. I like my clients to call on me; I'm the one who calls the insurance company and proves the case so that they can get the care that they need.

Nobody wants to think about these things, but the truth is that there are only two things that are going to happen to people. They're either going to need long-term care of some sort—which means they're having troubles with two out of the six activities of daily living and they need what is called custodial care—or they're going to just pass away. Those are two huge contingencies.

Nursing home care is incredibly expensive. Home health care is also expensive. I understand that people want to stay at home. At least 85 percent of my clients have told me that if they can't manage the six activities of daily living—eating, bathing, getting dressed, toileting, transferring, and continence—they still want to stay in their home. So any plan we make for retirement has to include that possibility.

I work with my clients to show them ways to use their savings to provide for any long-term care needs. We can take some of that money, that's maybe just sitting in a bank account collecting only 0.13.percent, and put it into what's called a single premium contract. They can use the death benefit of that contract for purposes of long-term care, and if they don't use it for long-term care, the money can be passed to their beneficiary tax-free passing outside of probate.

The Perils of Inflation, or Lasagna and Chocolate Cake

There's one more factor that can affect the decision on when to retire, and that is inflation. It's critically important to understand what inflation does to everyone's money, and it's something we don't talk about enough.

Inflation is about the purchasing power of a dollar. We all know that a dollar isn't what it used to be, but we seldom talk about exactly how much it has eroded.

Let me give you an example from my own life.

I was born in 1960, and on my 11th birthday in 1971 my mom made me a special dinner with my favorite foods, lasagna and chocolate cake. I remember her going to the grocery store with $100 that my dad had given her, and with that $100 she filled a whole shopping cart with all the ingredients for my birthday dinner and much more.

That same $100 dollars today certainly would not fill a grocery cart. It wouldn't even pay for lasagna and chocolate cake. According to the Bureau of Labor Statistics, prices in 2020 are 538.71 percent higher than they were in 1971. That means that $100 worth of groceries in 1971 would cost $638.71 today.

Inflation has been running a little over three and a half percent. So if you're not making a minimum of three and a half percent on your money, you're not even keeping up with today's inflation. So that's one more factor we need to include as we calculate the cost to be you in retirement and determine when you choose to retire.

All of these factors—pension, Social Security, taxes, savings, long-term care, longevity, inflation—have a role in making your retirement plan and determining when you can retire. As a chartered retirement planning counselor, I want to help my clients do the planning they need so that they can go out and enjoy their life to the full for as long as they can. When they reach the No-Go years, and they're rarely leaving their home, I want them to look back and say, "We did the planning and we had all those wonderful times and we have no regrets." That's really what it's all about, and I've seen it time and time again.

Chapter Four

How to Retire

You've thought about why you want to retire, and you've decided when you want to retire. So now it's time to look at the nuts and bolts of <u>how</u> to retire. What are the plans you need to make and the steps you need to take?

Retirement planning is about being prepared for whatever may come.

When I talk about this in my seminars, I like to use the example of the *Titanic*. As everyone knows from their history books—or at least from the movie—the RMS *Titanic* was on its maiden voyage from England to New York when it hit an iceberg and sank off the coast of Newfoundland on April 15, 1912. It was one of the worst maritime tragedies in history, killing 1,517 people.

The *Titanic* was designed to be the largest and most luxurious cruise ship in the world. It was also one of the fastest, and its design was supposed to make it virtually unsinkable. What could possibly go wrong?

Of course, it turned out that everything could go wrong. That "unsinkable" design turned out to have a fatal flaw. And the ship only had lifeboats enough for 1,178 people, although the ship itself could accommodate up to 2,435 passengers and

900 crew members. Even under the best of circumstances, the lifeboats would only be able to carry about a third of the people on board.

The *Titanic* tragedy was a masterpiece in failing to plan. You might even call it a prime example of how not to plan.

What does all this have to do with how to retire? The lesson that we can take from the story of the *Titanic* is to be prepared for the unexpected. In life, anything can happen. You never know exactly what to expect. There are things you can anticipate, but life also throws curve balls and you need to be ready to hit them.

That's where I come in. Over 27 years of helping people plan for successful retirement, I have seen just about every one of those curve balls, and I can help you hit them. I can help you plan for any contingency.

I've heard it over and over again: "Oh my God, I never thought that would happen." But things <u>do</u> happen. Kids and grandkids need help. Elderly parents need help. People in the sandwich generation find themselves helping both kids <u>and</u> parents. Things happen, and everything that happens costs money. My goal in planning to help make sure that there are no financial surprises when the unexpected happens. We always make a backup plan. I call it my conceptual contingency planning.

This is Not Your Grandfather's Retirement

In the last chapter I told the story of my grandpa Hank, who retired with a party, a gold watch, and a pension. That was typical for my grandpa's day; it's not typical today.

Retirement has changed. We used to talk about something called the three-legged stool of retirement. The three legs of the stool were one's pension, Social Security, and personal savings.

But in the '80s, during the Reagan administration, there were changes in the law that made it more attractive for employers to change the way they provided for their employees' retirement. Instead of offering <u>defined benefit</u> plans, like pensions, employers began offering what are called <u>defined contribution</u> plans, such as a 401(k) or 403(b).

With a defined benefit plan, the employer promises the employee a certain amount of money upon retirement. The employer has to set that money aside and manage it to ensure that there will be enough money to pay retirees their agreed-upon pension.

Employers prefer defined contribution plans because they don't have to worry about managing their employees' retirement funds. They just make their contribution—often matching what the employee contributes—but the responsibility for managing the account falls on the employee. While it is supposed to take the place of a pension, it actually functions as a sort of do-it-yourself retirement account.

But most working people are not stock market experts or mutual fund experts. They're busy working every day and maybe raising a family; they don't have the time or financial expertise to manage their 401(k) well. It can be really overwhelming.

I sit down with my clients and take the time to explain what a 401(k) is, how to work with it, and what they can do with it after they stop working.

The New Three-Legged Stool

Since pensions have almost disappeared, the old three-legged stool has been reduced to a two-legged one, just Social Security and personal savings, which includes any 401(k) accounts. And a two-legged stool just isn't going to stand on its own.

The good news is that in my role as a chartered retirement planning counselor, I can be the new third leg of the stool. You can count on me to help make your retirement stand.

You can count on my nearly 30 years of experience working with clients and walking them through all the steps of creating a successful retirement. I know how to do this and I can help you learn how to do it too.

Taking Inventory

Our starting point is always taking inventory. Yes, that means a financial inventory—what money you have, where it is, how it is placed—but that is only the start. When I work with clients, financial inventory is only a piece of the puzzle. We also take inventory of your goals, your wishes, your bucket list. And one of the most important questions I always ask is this: What are your fears?

Understanding people's financial fears helps me get right to the heart of the matter by addressing those fears immediately and directly. I can go right to the source and say, "If these are your fears, one, two, and three, let's face those first because then you can really just relax and listen."

Taking your financial inventory means figuring out what we have to work with. That includes a pension if you have one, your estimated Social Security benefit, your 401(k) or similar accounts, any emergency funds in savings, maybe even any inheritance you might anticipate receiving.

We use that financial inventory to develop the first essential part of your retirement plan, which is your income plan. What I do is draw two big circles on the my notepad, and as I list the items in the inventory I separate them into what I call the qualified bucket and the non-qualified bucket. It's important to make that distinction, because qualified money and non-qualified money are taxed differently. We look at those two buckets and figure out what we need to take out and when we need to take it out in order to satisfy your income need.

Your qualified money is money that has never been taxed. This includes tax-deferred money like your 401(k), for example. When you start using that money, you will have to pay taxes on it, so we need to take that into account in your income plan.

What You Don't Know About Your 401(k) Can Hurt You

As we said before, pensions have largely been replaced by defined contribution plans like 401(k)s. Even though these plans are so common, I find they are not well understood, so it's worth taking a closer look.

The typical 401(k) actually includes three types of money. The first is your own pretax contribution, which is the amount you choose to have deducted from your paycheck prior to taxes. The second is your employer's contribution, often some kind of a match on your own contribution. And the third, hopefully, is any gain that the account makes over time. What you need to understand is that <u>all</u> of that money is 100 percent taxable. That's a very important point to remember. These are tax-<u>deferred</u> accounts, not tax-free accounts. The idea behind this is the expectation that once you retire, you will be in a lower tax bracket, so you defer paying taxes on some of the money you make during your highest tax bracket years until you reach that lower tax bracket.

If you have a 401(k) or similar account, you regularly receive a statement showing the return on that account. What you need to understand about that is the difference between the <u>average</u> return and the <u>actual</u> return. They are not necessarily the same.

Here's a simple example: Let's suppose you have $1,000 in an account. You lose 50 percent of it one year because of a drop in the market, so now you're down to $500. The next year is a good one and you make a 50 percent gain, but a 50 percent gain doesn't get you back to where you started, because 50 percent gain on $500 means you only have $750. For those two years, your average return is zero, but your actual return is negative 25 percent. In another example, if you lose 30 percent on your money one year, you need to make 43 percent to get back to where you started. Of course, if you never experience a negative return, your average return will always equal your actual return, but over a number of years that's unlikely.

Now let's take it a step further and look at the return over a period of years. This is where you run into something called the <u>sequence of returns</u>, and it's something we need to consider for retirement income planning. If your account takes a significant drop close to your retirement, or even after you have retired, you have much less time to recover from that drop. If you need a recent example, just look at the aftermath of the financial crisis of 2008. Many people lost huge sums from their retirement savings, and it took them many years just to recoup what they lost, never mind making any gain.

All of this explains why we have to look carefully at your 401(k) account (or accounts, if you have more than one) in creating your income plan. After all, did we ever think our lives would change so drastically from a virus? My clients never lost a penny on their investments we established together.

Determining the Cost to Be You—and How to Pay It

Learning how to retire is about determining the income that you will need and how to create a secure, guaranteed income using the contents of your financial inventory.

When they retire, most people are not going to need lump sums of money, but 99.9 percent are going to need income. The cost to be you in retirement is the monthly income that you need to maintain your lifestyle and meet your goals. We look at your secure income—that is your pension, if you have one, and your Social Security—and then calculate any difference between that secure income and the cost to be you.

When I work with clients, I show them examples of when, how, and why we're going to take their money—both their qualified money and their non-qualified money—and put together a plan by taking systematic penalty-free withdrawals from different monies. This is the basis of an income plan which will eventually be one piece of the jigsaw puzzle that includes a tax plan, a healthcare plan, and a risk management plan.

As we build the income plan, we'll look at some of the decisions we discussed earlier, like pension options and Social Security choices. I like to lay out all of the options for my clients so that they can make informed decisions.

There are also some specifics about what to do with your 401(k) and IRA. These accounts have what are called required minimum distributions (RMDs), meaning that you have to start withdrawing a minimum amount once you reach a certain age. The good news for you is that thanks to a very recent change in the law—the SECURE Act, passed in December 2019—the age for taking RMDs has been pushed back from 70 and a half to 72. That gives you more time to let that money build up and possibly convert some of it to tax-free money.

While you are still working, you can take advantage of a wonderful program called an in-service 401(k) rollover, which allows you to take a large chunk of your 401(k) and roll it into a position where you cannot lose.

When people retire, I encourage them to roll their 401(k) into an IRA. Once they are retired, they are no longer contributing to that account via payroll deduction, they have very little control over the account, and they're no longer around their co-workers sharing information. There are no more water-cooler conversations in the office saying, "How did your 401(k) do?" Once you're retired and you're sitting on the shore of a lake fishing, there's no reason why you should leave your money with your former employer where no one's looking at it.

When you roll that money into what is basically a self-directed IRA, guess who's looking at it? I am. I'm figuring out all the different moving parts of your IRA—what indexes they're in, what the caps are, what your participation rates are, what the spreads are—and any changes that need to be made to protect your retirement.

In going from a 401(k) into an IRA we do what's called a direct transfer, which is a nontaxable event. When you roll your 401(k) into an IRA, you can just let the money grow, and not take it until you have to take your RMD at age 72. In some circumstances you can also take some money—a certain percentage each year—and convert it into a Roth IRA, which is tax free. But remember, everything that we do with your qualified 401(k) plan has to do with what your income needs are, and your income needs may not allow for a Roth conversion.

It may be that your number one concern is just taking advantage of the chance that this can generate an income. The best scenario is this: Making enough money with no downside risk to allow you to take an income or to allow you to take your required minimum distribution.

The longer that you can preserve your principal, the better. I show my clients various options and talk with them not only about what's going to happen at the beginning of their retirement, but also what might happen throughout the course of their retirement. I always remind them that retirement is a marathon, not a sprint.

Managing Risk

One more extremely important piece of the overall retirement plan is a risk management plan. As I pointed out earlier in this book, retirement is the longest period of unemployment in your lifetime.

To have a successful retirement, you need to understand risk and you have to plan for contingencies. Losing money could truly derail your retirement success, so you need to make sure you're not going backwards. You need to avoid taking market losses, paying fees and commissions, and being in the wrong income plan.

In today's financial environment, there is no monopoly on good ideas. It's important to get a second opinion and to find out what prudent and informed investors are doing with their money. One of the things I always tell people when they're investing with me is this: Never underestimate the power of zero.

What do I mean by that? Imagine that you were to go to Las Vegas and play blackjack, where for every hand that you play, you get to keep the money when you win and never lose money when you lose. You always break even. That's the kind of planning that I do—if the market does well, you enjoy the gain, but if the market doesn't do well, you may not make any, but you're not going to lose any. That's the power of zero.

Putting the Puzzle Together

All of these elements—the income plan, the tax plan, the healthcare plan, and the risk management plan—fit together just like puzzle pieces to create your successful retirement. But each of these elements involves critical decisions that affect the rest of your life. These decisions will affect your spouse's life, they will affect any legacy you want to leave to your children or to charity, and any other life goals you may have.

None of this is easy, but the good news is that you don't have to go it alone. You don't have to become a retirement expert; you can rely on a chartered retirement planning counselor like me to serve as that essential third leg of your retirement stool.

Whatever your line of work, throughout your working life you keep learning. There are always new technologies, new procedures, new ways of doing things. Over the years you become an expert at what you do. Think of all the things you've learned and all the experience you've gained in your working years. Don't you deserve to have that kind of expertise at hand in your retirement? Don't you deserve help from someone who has spent their whole career gaining that expertise?

Success Stories

All those years ago when I started my company, I named it Successful Seniors because that was my goal—to help retirees have the same kind of safe, successful retirement that my grandpa Hank had. My grandpa was able to spend his days fly fishing, something he always loved. And my dad was able to get in as much golf as he wanted. They both inspired me in the way they approached retirement.

After nearly 30 years of doing this, I can point to many similar stories among my own clients. Let me tell you about a couple of them.

Bob and Janet have been with me for many years. When I first started working with them, they were just starting to see the light at the end of the tunnel in approaching retirement. They had always believed in the stock market. I had only been in the business for a few years, but even back then I pointed out that since they were getting ready to retire, they could not afford to lose any money. I counseled them to take a commonsense approach by looking at some of the fixed situations, and they trusted me to help them do that. I remember the appointment well. I remember what I asked them to do, I remember the expression that they gave me when I asked them to do it, and they did it.

More than 20 years later, Bob and Janet are still with me. They still have that same product that I recommended, and they're still taking income from it. And they're still hunting. They're still fishing. They still like to rent a boat to go to Alaska and catch halibut. And when they do, they still give me some of the halibut they catch, which is great. It always makes me smile to see them; they're two of my most successful seniors.

One of my other favorite clients is Joe. He spent 40 years as an airplane engineer and his retirement plan was challenging. Over the years his employer, like so many other companies, kept changing their pension plan and kept changing all the incentives they offered to retain employees. So by the time Joe was ready to retire, he'd had three or four different pension plans.

When you are in a situation like that, it's very important to understand how all of those work, what your options are, which ones are taxable, and which ones are maybe after-tax monies. But when you're leaving a large company like Joe was, you're going to walk into a human resource person who's going to present you with options for how to retire.

In Joe's case, the HR person said there were three different options. One, Joe could take 100 percent of your pension and leave his spouse nothing if he were to die. Two, he could defer 15 percent of his pension and leave his spouse 50 percent of what he would receive? Or three, he could defer 25 percent of his pension, and then when he passed away, his wife would receive his same pension for the rest of her life. Of course, if Joe deferred part of his pension and his wife were to predecease him, the company would get to keep the deferred money. Well, Joe had worked his way up to senior management and stood to receive a massive pension. If his wife were to die first, Joe would lose hundreds of thousands of dollars. He wanted to provide for his wife, but how could he avoid that loss?

Well, there are ways to avoid it, but it takes some intricate planning. We look at various tools to combat this issue, some of which have to do with the health and longevity of both the husband and wife. We look at a lot of different factors to make a decision like this. It didn't matter that Joe had given them 40 years; the HR person wanted him to make this huge decision in about 25 minutes. Because Joe and I had done the preparation, Joe was able to keep 100 percent of his pension and still provide for his wife. In a situation like that, you need to go in there with all of your ducks in a row and completely prepared on what you want to do, so that you are sure of making the right decision. If you don't, you risk being intimidated by the HR department that is motivated to keep as much money as possible within the company. But that shouldn't be even an issue if you've done the proper planning; you should be entitled to everything that you have worked for.

It all comes back to education and preparation. It comes back to looking at an individual's particular situation and figuring out what it is that you want to do. That's my job.

That's why, after you read this book and we have an appointment, I'm going to be on your side. I'm going to be working with you and educating you so that you make all these decisions in your best interest. Not in my best interests, and not in the best interest of the company that you gave 40 years of work to, but in your best interest.

I promise that the things I'm going to do with your money in retirement are the things that I'm doing with my own money. I own every product that I have ever sold. I think that's important for an advisor, because if you don't own the product, you have no skin in the game. I don't think I have a right to give people advice that I don't take myself. That's very important to me.

I'm trying to be as successful as I can with not only my own portfolio but with yours. Because when you do well, you know that I'm doing the same. And when I do well, I know you're going to do the same.

Age has taught me that what other people think of me is none of my business.

Chapter Five

Next Step: Let's Talk

Now that we have looked at the why, when, and how of retirement, it's time to talk about the next step, which is up to you.

I understand that thinking about retirement can be overwhelming. I understand those feelings of fear and anxiety, and I know those feelings make it easy to procrastinate. I hope this book has helped to start easing some of those fears and make it easier for you to take that next step of talking to an advisor.

A Typical Appointment

When we schedule a first appointment, I always like to get together at some kind of casual meeting spot instead of my office. I like to just buy people a cup of coffee.

I typically show up a little bit early so I can get a private corner table. I'll offer to buy a coffee and maybe a bite to eat, so we can break bread together and get acquainted. It's a chance for the person to get to know me a bit and for me to start learning their story.

Everyone has a story, and getting to hear those stories is one of my favorite aspects of my job. I just let my guest tell me their story. I want to hear about their family, their work, and the kind of things they like to do. I also explain a little about myself and give them an opportunity to ask any initial questions they might have for me. This first meeting is about getting comfortable and allaying any fears or hesitation.

There are some common questions I'm frequently asked, like how long have I been in the area, how long I've been in the business, and how I get paid. Just the other day I had someone ask me, "How do we get to the situation where you'll take us on as clients?" And what I told him was, "Well, you had come to my workshop and you have this need, and I am constantly looking for wonderful folks like you to work with."

As for how I get paid, I never charge any fees or commissions; I'm not even licensed anymore to do that. When I provide clients with a product, 100 percent of the time I am compensated by the company. I tell people I get paid two ways. I get paid not only when they initially move money, but also every year that they stay happy. That's one more reason why it's very important for me to provide excellent service.

Usually an hour just flies right by, and then I'll ask about meeting again, maybe a couple of weeks later, again just getting together for coffee. It's not really a second appointment; it's more like part two of our first meeting. But I always make it clear that there is never any obligation for them to work with me. I'm not the kind of advisor who asks for fees and commissions, and I never want my clients to feel obligated.

At that second meeting we'll start gathering an inventory, as we talked about in the last chapter. We'll talk about goals, bucket lists, and resources. We'll start looking at finances—what money the individual has and how it is placed. I'll ask them to explain their understanding of how their money is working, and I may point out that there may be a better way. Other times, I'm able to tell them that I think what they're doing is great.

Some people like to look at their investments every day on an online brokerage account. For them it's almost a hobby, and if that's the case, I afford them the opportunity to keep doing that. But I also explain to them the importance of safe money. I like to call it sleep insurance because they have the ability to go to bed every night knowing that their income plan is going to be there.

So a typical appointment usually lasts between one and two hours, over one or two meetings. Afterward, I invite the individual to reach out to me at their convenience. I give them my cell phone number, my email address, my website, and various ways for them to connect with me.

I love being able to help people, and always enjoy meeting with new folks. It's a privilege to hear their stories, and I look forward to hearing yours. Call me—let's talk!

Growing older is a precious commodity. Only a few can endure to achieve that distinguished distinction and quality.

Conclusion

THANK YOU SO MUCH for reading this book. I hope you have found it helpful and I encourage you to reach out to me to make an appointment—no obligation, no strings attached.

I consider education to be an important part of my work. When the subject of retirement comes up at your next family gathering, or office party, or picnic with friends, I hope that this book will make it possible for you to help your friends and family understand the real cost to be you in retirement.

If you have friends or family members you think would benefit from reading this book, please let me know; I would be happy to offer them a copy. I am always grateful for referrals.

About the Author

DOUGLAS W. FAIR, JD, CRPC
Doug is the owner and founder of Successful Seniors. For more than 27 years, he has dedicated his career to working with hundreds of individuals to help them succeed in retirement.

He is a graduate of Vanderbilt University and in 1988 he received his law degree.

In 2020 Doug received a Lifetime Achievement Award from Aegis Financial for his outstanding contributions, unwavering loyalty, and commitment to excellence. Doug plans on dedicating another 25 years to seniors looking for success in all their remaining years.

Doug and his wife Claudine have three daughters and enjoy a full life in the beautiful city of Colorado Springs, Colorado.

www.ExpertPress.net

Made in the USA
Columbia, SC
25 February 2025

54394309R00035